FIVE FOR NOTHING

Copyright © Cindy King 2025
All rights reserved

First Published by Galileo Press in 2025
Aiken, South Carolina

ISBN: 978-0-913123-53-9

Please visit freegalileo.com

Cover Art: Stephen Reichert, *A Formal Invitation to Arson*
(2019, oil on wood pulp paper)
Book Design: Adam Robinson for goodbookdevelopers.com

FIVE FOR NOTHING

Cindy King

GALILEO PRESS
Aiken, South Carolina

Grateful acknowledgment to the following publications where poems from this collection are forthcoming or first appeared:

Antioch Review
Baltimore Review
Cincinnati Review
Cola Literary Review
Copper Nickel
Denver Quarterly
DIAGRAM
The Fiddlehead
Frontier Poetry
Gettysburg Review
The McNeese Review
Midwest Quarterly
The Minnesota Review
The Missouri Review
New American Writing
New England Review
North American Review
Plume
Prairie Schooner
Poet Lore
Redivider
The South Carolina Review
So to Speak
Sou'wester
The Threepenny Review
TriQuarterly
Verse Daily

CONTENTS

Behind the Wheel | 1
Night Shift | 2
Noumenon | 3
Misdirection | 4
Anamnesis | 5
Happy Hour | 6
Fault (after Harryette Mullen) | 7
Elegy for a Eulogy | 8
Animus | 9
Corpus | 10
Mortality Forward, Mortality on the Nose | 11
Know Your Place: Disco Edition | 13
Possession | 14
No Will | 16
Matrons of the Ward | 18
Capacitor (Be Mine) | 19
Flake | 20
Spring and All, Etc. | 22
Daily Affirvotions | 23
Crescendo | 24
A Poem by Dean Young by Mary Ruefle by Cindy King | 25
It's Either That, or You're Pregnant Again | 26
Mis- | 27
Vive les Vampires | 28
Man vs. Himself | 30
The Governor Asks Us to Pray for Rain | 31
Rave On | 32
No Context | 33

BEHIND THE WHEEL

The therapist asks me a question,
and I don't know the answer.
I suspect she knows because
she knows me better than
I know what's under the hood.
I have given her the keys
to my inner Ferrari, so she drives
recklessly down the treacherous
coastal highway of our weekly grand prix.
I open my mouth. No words.
My tongue backed into the garage
of my throat, where it idles,
then stalls and fails to turn over.
I hold a can to my lips
and hope that it is gasoline.
The therapist repeats the question,
and I lose control of my leg.
It skidders and shakes—no brakes
for the unbalanced thigh.
I stare at the door
like it's a windscreen,
see through to the receptionist,
buffing her fingernails
as if this were a body shop,
not one repairing heads.
Tonight, she'll be driving,
top down, with her friends,
where the answers bloom like wildflowers,
beyond the road's soft shoulders.

NIGHT SHIFT

I start listening to houseplants,
learn their dead languages.
A fly lands in my soup
and I eat around it
until the bowl is empty.
Everyone loses something eventually.
My neck carries the weight of my head,
buckling with what lives there.
The withered mouth of
the philodendron
smiling broadly.
In the middle of the night
I replace the batteries
of the TV remote
that has been so faithful
and patient with me.
Across the alley in the shop
of the garment maker,
a hundred hands stitch trim
onto jackets, sew sleeves
to shoulders, steam creases
and seams. While I lie awake
in television light,
waiting for the night to end,
and for the third-shift mothers
to be returned to their children.

NOUMENON

The bed was thus, the curtains were therefore.
The moon floated past the window frame
and appeared to be. Fans roared as softly as.
A blue light becoming, or a wind
unlike anything outside.
Or a memory of, but less than.
A fine dust settling on the dust ruffle.
Released from memory. Released into remembering.
Motor coach and reservoir, children and fools.
The pasture being itself, in other words, midnight, perfume.
Schopenhauer breathing into a paper bag.
Sequins, rutabaga, emerald hills.
Burj Khalifa and a feeling
that in a moment anything could.
That the clouds might.
4:00 p.m. Al Ain: what to say?
Or your voice, the risk of. And rebar.
Then traffic, rushing as if it could stop.
Sure it could.
The noise, the ticking. Noise,
noise, boom. You letting go
was unlike. You leaving
was nearly like.

MISDIRECTION

> When love is gone, there's always justice.
> And when justice is gone, there's always force.
> And when force is gone, there's always Mom. Hi Mom!
> —Laurie Anderson

Nevertheless, the tooth my brother placed
beneath his pillow remained, all night,
and the next, and the one after that, unmoved.
Ditto for the milk and cookies we left for Santa.
Flash forward: After the earthquake, my brother
inspects an overpass for structural damage, and
I meet with a student approximately 1,986 miles away.
He's failing my class, he says, because he's cheating on his girlfriend.
Meanwhile, the governor of Alabama (initially advocating for a surgical approach)
signs a bill calling for chemical castration.
Next up: sterilization for deadbeat dads?

So yeah, there's still no light in the attic. But no worries,
the fire's burning on the other side of the house;
the water has only risen to the windows (the tornado's *waaay* down the street).
At the zoological museum, there's a scorpion suspended
in amber. Could it wait another millennium to sting?
As for the rats, ticks, and roaches, we could just as well see those at home.
Of extinction, what's not to love?
Who will mourn the pubic lice
in the ongoing war against body hair?
Could it be that it all boils down to what Laurie
Anderson said about love and justice? Like the last time
I saw my father on a gurney behind glass. Or the way I refuse
Communion: fingers curled into fists, arms crossed,
x-ing out the thumping thing that failed him,
but is keeping me alive.

ANAMNESIS

I remember the last time I had fish.
It was at a waterfront restaurant
with my mother.
I ordered a cocktail.
My mother brought her own—
a pharmacological rainbow
she shook from what looked to me
like a little plastic coffin.
It was a Saturday or Sunday
when the fish was placed before me,
and when I ran my knife down
the silver length of its body,
it opened its mouth.
Sit up straight, I heard it say,
and elbows off the table—
though that was decades ago
and it could have come
from my mother's mouth.
My mother is a fish now, like
the one in the Faulkner novel.
You are what you eat, they say.
I have become a vegetarian
instead of becoming my mother.

HAPPY HOUR

I've never been known for my ability to see into the future.
I drank in the superficial darkness of a 4:30 twilight
and thought something would happen.
This isn't to say I haven't got intuition.
It's possible I've been loitering too long
in the gingerbread kitchens of witches,
engaging in books with onionskin pages
and faulty spells for *happy* tears.
And then came a knock,
and then I ignored it.
And with a great deal of tenderness
I made peace with the door.
Could it be that I'm finally moving forward?
On my feet, cacti and foothills scroll beside me,
but the ground where I stand remains still.
And with some clairvoyance, I see you on your feet,
legs moving you down a cobbled street in Paris or Bruges.
Though it could be that at this hour
you are sitting in your cinema of self-loathing,
playing and replaying a cringe reel:
    the great effort resulting in ridicule,
      the grand gesture that ended in rejection,
      the bold action that failed.
So, when you move it's with more noise than intended,
as if to flood the vast chasm of silence with sound,
like a witch in her kitchen—one younger, less warty,
who is shaking up a cocktail of alacrity and joy.

FAULT (AFTER HARRYETTE MULLEN)

If only she would have…didn't she know that…she should have…
why didn't she…how didn't she…how could she have…she was the
only one who…she should have known not to… she just shouldn't
have…she was way too…why wasn't she…she just didn't…
what was she…where were her…how could she…she might have
been…she didn't…how could she be so…didn't she realize…she
just wasn't…she didn't understand that…how could she not have
known that…why didn't she simply…she should have…if only…

ELEGY FOR A EULOGY

You asked me to deliver the eulogy
at Dad's memorial service
to spare the survivors of our family
the mortifying prospect of public speaking.
For five hours, I have flown above earth,
wordlessly, over Great Plains and Rocky Mountains.
Under a moon of reading light, I have learned
why no one ever calls it a light by which to write.
I have failed the galaxy, didn't listen to the stars.

I would have rather bought more lilies,
than to say what I remember,
brought another noodle casserole.
Let me rummage instead through your pantry, Mom,
tear wild violets from your yard.
But please, don't ask me to see him from a distance,
to view him with a naked eye, to show
him as a moon, without blemish,
free of rilles, scars, dark sides.

ANIMUS

When I imagine him in the afterlife,
my dad haggles with the ferryman,
refuses the ride across the river
and chooses instead to swim.
At the gates of heaven, he won't
give his name, demands to speak
with God himself, as if God were
the general manager, the senior
supervisor of the universe.
On the muddy banks
of the river of forgetfulness,
he chugs the murky water.
I wonder if in here, in the hereafter,
he still remembers me.

I'm not sure what the animals think
when they see him in his stiff white coat,
wandering the fields of Elysium.
Do they sniff the air and trot away coolly,
or come to lick his palm?
A long look, I should think,
could call beasts back into the wild,
drive out any trace of domestication.
What words would they have for the man
who butchered them,
whose sacrifice filled our family's plates—
rosy ham, leg of lamb bouquet?
What lessons in magnanimity and forgiveness?

CORPUS

When you finish burning, what's left
sends a black thread of smoke
through fresh ash like a hand
waving the last of us away.
You didn't ask to return.
If you did, God never answered,
passing your request to some minor deity,
some lesser bird of paradise.
Nonetheless, you're here,
your body the shape of a milk snake,
whale shark, dust devil—
something only appearing to be dangerous.
Alive, we knew you as a closed door,
the sound of crushed gravel, a truck
backing down the drive. For how long
did I mistake you for night,
a dog's bark, an owl?
Now, we've packed up cold cuts,
hung dress clothes, and didn't sing.
Though we'd rather sleep,
we drink whisky in the backyard.
But still, here you are, failed storm,
waterspout, empty threat that's not quite done with us.

MORTALITY FORWARD, MORTALITY ON THE NOSE

Sunshine. Everyday, sun. A thrust through
the turnstile to the unforgiving heaven, desert of forgetting—
your childhood, adolescence, most of your adult life.

The walk in the park, not much mortality in that.
You need fitness—heart, lungs, abs.
The other list: cigarettes, antidepressants, box wine,
all those micro-mortalities accumulate in the bloodstream.

Didn't you ask? You didn't ask. My father died last year.
He was a butcher; Hell is for vegans.
Those pink rocks looks just like pork chops.
I know all about his *I-told-you-so*'s, nothing of your *I'm-so-sorries*.

I keep walking in sunshine. No prophesies
required. No sunscreen or shade.
Crosswalk. White light. Man made of stars.
The RV that nearly hit me. *Murderers*,
I shout from the middle of the street.
Oh, if only I had a teenager to be ashamed of
me, to see his mother, sultana in cheap sneakers.

My father used to say, *Clean your plate. God put animals on earth for us to eat.*
Who's eating them now? What's eating him?

God, what gives? Cleanliness isn't godliness anymore.
Is there a he, she, or it (anyone) at the end of this goddamned prayer line?
My dad, he'd pick up if he had a phone down there.
As it was, his last pro-mortality, a burger he ate
with my ghost child. Offspring of a nine-month pregnancy scare,
eating with my father.

Fear is to rage what blade is to whetting stone,
shame the utensil he most avoided.
Regret a carcass dismembered.

Drumstick, music, with something he'd fill my plate.

My mother tells me he wasn't drafted, he
enlisted in the army at the height of the War.
He wanted to kill, she says.
He wanted to go to college.

KNOW YOUR PLACE: DISCO EDITION

I feel really dumb at the nightclub
wearing pink vinyl pants with sensible shoes,
compression socks with a red velvet corset,
bifocals and borrowed biker jacket.
A bad place to bring a cat,
same goes for a headache.
Ditto for a cup of herbal tea
and a copy of the Old Testament.
A mirror ball rotates above the dance floor,
fracturing light into unholy pieces,
the perfect planet for narcissists
if it weren't too small for all of us
to make of it our home.

POSSESSION

Open package
Remove Styrofoam
Discard Styrofoam
Do not eat Styrofoam
Keep staples from wrists
Keep staples from eyes
Remove all parts: base, top, shelves, dowels, anxiety, screws, nail holder, nails, rage, brackets, back panel, these instructions (you've done that), depression, espresso-colored stickers, cat standing on package
Place items on carpet (no carpet)
Place items on scratch-free surface (not beneath cat)
Gather shelves into one area
Gather hardware into another
Everything will appear to be hardware
Everything has potential to scratch
Find hammer
Keep hammer away from head
Keep hammer away from heads of others
Find screwdriver
Find it is the wrong kind
Cry into hands
Try not to cry into hands
Try not to cry
Try never to cry again
Attach sides to base with wooden dowels
(What are dowels?)
The only items from package made from actual wood
Withhold judgment
Attach top to base
See frame wobble
See frame collapse
Repeat previous steps
Not all steps, only those necessary
(What is necessary?)
That which eliminates wobble
That which prevents collapse
Do not eat Styrofoam

Keep staples from wrists
Force screws into predrilled holes
Not those predrilled holes
The other ones
Start by using fingers
Feel screws bite skin
Finish with screwdriver (still the wrong kind)
Unfold back panel
Yes, it is not one piece
Yes, it is held together with packing tape
Withhold judgment
Resist impulse to quit
Repress urge to give up
Use tape measure…
Search for tape measure…
Search for tape measure…
Search for tape measure…
Using your judgment (you may judge now)
Position back panel
Do not use tape
Attach to frame with nails at even intervals
Even intervals
Use nail holder
Not fingers
Use nail holder
There should be no leftover nails
(There are leftover nails)
Place shelf pins in predrilled holes
Yes, those holes
Shelves should not slope
Shelves should be even
Shelves should not slide out onto scratch-free surface
Position bookcase in bedroom
Unpack box labeled "Tom's Books"
Unpack box labeled "Mine"
Forget difference
Forget distinction
Shelve together
Books, bookshelves, espresso-colored stickers
Everything is yours

NO WILL

You won't be prepared for the probate lawyer,
who'll fail to find in his heart's budget,
water or tissues for tears.
From all accounts in his economy, neither
has ever returned the beloved.

No one will mention the traffic downtown,
warn of five-car collisions, overturned
semis and minivans in flames.

At the justice end of Commerce Street,
they won't make it clear
that your car will be met with barricades.
No one will say where to park near the courthouse,
no mention of meters or need for change.

They won't say how you'll sleepwalk through sprinklers,
sink into earth by your heels.
It won't be disclosed why when crossing the street,
you can't be bothered to look both ways.

You won't know that you'll want to ask the man
behind yellow tape why he jumped
on *this* of all mornings, from *this* of all buildings
so near your destination.
You won't care to know the source of his suffering,
or what could've been done to have stopped him.

You won't be told that the judge will be late—
no excuse or apology—
When he'll finally appear, nobody'll say
that you'll still be expected to rise.

No one will say of the courtroom,
it belongs in an old Hollywood film—
all polished wood and windows that span
from floor to ceiling.

The afternoon light won't be explained,
how it'll be softened by sheers.
No one will tell you you'll see nothing as beautiful,
like you did the time before.

MATRONS OF THE WARD

A widow is sentenced up to fifteen years
after the departure of her beloved
to sleep with his clothes: the happier
the marriage, the more complete
her rehabilitation. Our institutions
aim to protect the public after all.
Iron Lady is a film about rust.
And the one on disarmament is *Annie Get Your Gun*.
The moon never asked for "Clair de Lune."
The moon was, well, famous before.
A woman must share her story as if every man
has lived it in the great, grand history of the world.
If only she could tell it in a way that those who heard it
would literally explode—or spark just a bit,
then leap overboard. Unremarkable still that a woman
has never been known for sawing a man in two. Or for freeing
herself from a straitjacket while chained to the floor of the ocean.

CAPACITOR (BE MINE)

Call us anything: *spirits, specters, spooks*—
Say what you will about ghosts & widows:
that we don't exist, we're invisible,
that we go naked under the sheets,
and leave pornography in little free libraries.

Oh, how we messed with Ms. O'Keeffe
until she ditched mimesis for yonic flowers—
Sweet ruin of a decaying arrangement,
biological clock shocked by the red pulse of time…

Oh, how we would take your camera
and keep it on the nightstand
next to our bed. How we would take you
in your Subaru, between dashboard
and bucket seats—despite red dirt
                and lousy music.

Serendipity, acne, nothing connecting to nothing.
Poltergeistly, wet-palmed, the mopey joy
of mumbling the same words
because they never come out quite right.

Pretty much everything moves at erosion speed;
those blemishes on the blue sky are called *clouds*.
The world's mostly tweetups, irreconcilable
differences, legal separations, and restraining orders.
Forever after, the taxes happily unprepared. Our backs
bent beautifully like the workers at fulfillment centers.

Everyone's always endorsing accuracy over precision—
closeness of the measurements to a specific value,
over closeness of the measurements to each other.
Arrows missing hearts, bypassing bodies altogether.
(Would it help to get a bow?)
Or should we keep throwing them
and throwing: everly happy, everly after.

FLAKE

Yeah, there were things I didn't know,
like how you're not supposed to give newborns water,
run your car with the garage door closed.
How you're not supposed to drive 2,000 miles
on a spare tire, or how a lost filling
becomes a broken tooth, then no tooth at all.
And how loving someone to the exclusion
of all others is always a bad idea.
Like the joke hiding in the Rothko,
like the alarm clock in your neighbor's
apartment you hear each day at 6:00 a.m.
Don't put butter on a fever.
Starve a burn, feed an abstract expressionist.
Some truths are best untold.
The answer to the question is liverwurst.
Many a great man's face has been stamped
on currency that's now worthless.
Don't microwave melamine. It is an artifact of the 1960s.
I too am an artifact. Just as the pharaoh
became an artifact when he was lifted from sand.
And you're surprised he was autophobic
and buried with his concubines?
My heart is made of shale.
I heard a meadowlark singing and asked if she
would move in with me. She may have said yes
if it weren't for that thing with the alarm clock.
It would seem, dear sir, that my credit score precedes me.
It will end in lost deposits—and quite possibly tears.
That zero in my brain is being seduced by a one.
My brain became a slow jam.
Let's get it on.
Then it switched stations and was wrapped in a prophylactic.
I was fixing a sandwich at the time.
We're not just taxpayers, we're all roses!
My brain was kicked by another brain,
which I borrowed from my neighbor (not, for the record, Mr. 6:00 a.m.).

Does anyone else ever think that the heart's too near the armpits?
Love stinks.
All hail the woman of shale.
It's just me.
We all think the best of each other, don't we,
especially those with guns in their glove box.
Some day that whimper will become a bang,
at least that's what they tell me,
and it won't be so easy to drown it out
with 90 decibels of R&B.
Here's the least, save the date, let's make it official.
Check out this invisible ink.
Be on the lookout for the woman of shale.
Cross my heart, hope to die,
this time, I swear, she's not me.

SPRING AND ALL, ETC.

I once met a man
five blocks from my apartment
by pretending I was lost.
His hair smelled of spring rain.
Did you ever fall asleep standing up?
At some point, we all had tails.
Even porcupines grow in wombs.
Even my cat knows what she wants
and how to get it, despite her limited
vocabulary, even if that thing is nothing
at all and she becomes a bowling ball
dropped onto my mattress when I'm trying to sleep.
Spring: forsythias simmer, froth—percolate?
Rain decides upon whom it will fall. Cherry blossoms
spread their bawdy propaganda.
Do caterpillar skins pulse with phantom wings?
Cicadas outgrow themselves, discard their bodies
like souls.
What do trees care for love?
They split, distort initials and hearts
we carve into their bark.
Yet it seems they know something about revenge.
Like the man who left me for a Google map
and found his way to the museum, where he discovered
that dinosaurs traveled in packs (social animals after all)
and were not the lonely, cold-blooded carnivores we'd imagined.
Take my word for it. You need not believe me.
Just look for yourself and see that everything
is purring and trilling and everlastingly soul twinned.
I once was lost, now I'm blind.
Remember: you are who you own.

DAILY AFFIRVOTIONS

Those pains in your chest aren't a heart attack, it's that bra you've been wearing since high school.

No, you're not fat, your friend's just built like a runway model.

That face you glimpsed in the storefront window, don't worry, it wasn't yours (and of course they sell those jeans in your size).

You look old in that picture only because you're holding a newborn. But no, no worries, that baby's not yours.

You're not pregnant for at least five different reasons. And certainly not, no, not one of them is menopause.

That's just a pimple, a hangnail, an ordinary mole.

Did you forget, you left your place a mess? No, you haven't been burglarized.

No one has used your credit card in El Paso; no one's charged a slushy, a Slim Jim, and 50 cartons of Winstons.

Yes, you spellchecked that message, changed *shits* to *shirts* before clicking send. And that letter, yes, it had plenty of postage; the receiver has just chosen not to reply.

Your car is in park, parking brake on. It has not rolled through the garage door, down the driveway, and out into the quiet street. No, your headlights aren't on.

Those are white hydrangeas, not doctors staked in the bushes. No, that's a unicorn, not a police car.

Relax, no one's looking at you. That fine young gentleman's not staring, he sees right through, to the unicorn standing behind you,

> and as for God, as for God you're good, God doesn't see you either.

CRESCENDO

Consent, however, there was never such a thing.
As if when a boy teased you, it only meant he liked you,
and if you teased back, you'd disappear. As if
being called *slut* made you taller,
and *whore* restored your voice—magic, see?
As if your fear of men could make you
walk on water, their touch could split you in half—
Long division (cherry pie filling), two selves never to meet again.
As if you could no longer breathe underwater,
surfacing no longer an option. You'd spit
and sputter and do the math. The equation adds up:
Asking for it + asking for it = deserving it. If A, then B.
Add. Subtract. Divide. Go forth, multiply.
Let them spin lead into gold,
speak secret names for God,
antiseptic, wind, water on your skin, eroding your hoodoo body…
It's all perfectly sane, normal even: predator/prey, Kingdom Animalia.
As if rape is never really rape,
as if you were quiet, quite quiet, then very, very loud.

A POEM BY DEAN YOUNG BY MARY RUEFLE BY CINDY KING

Assume for decades
I haven't suffered a cataclysmic,
life-altering event. A pregnancy, a loss,
an assault of any kind. The dog
in the raincoat is a global phenomenon,
an international incident, a cosmic,
seismic event. Doesn't believe in anxiety,
Doesn't believe in facial recognition software.
Assume I haven't seen bulls swabbed
onto cave walls. Assume I haven't tried the world's
most poisonous fish. Assume I have crushed,
then failed to resuscitate, the scorpion in my bathtub.
(I'm that kind of person.)
Assume I haven't burned an effigy of Renée Jeanne Falconetti.
Assume more than once I have sobbed in public places.
Of course, I've never painted a Pollock by numbers.
Many times have I never painted a Klein by the number
(the one corresponding with blue).
Never have I left a painting at your doorstep.
Never have I poured paint into your mouth.
Never have I died. Never, as a consequence, have I lived.
I'm sorry. No, I apologize. Someone told me
never to apologize for being late, but
to thank them, instead, for waiting.
Maybe now the neighboring countries
can live in peace and the dead can return
as starlings and gather in the evening sky.

IT'S EITHER THAT, OR YOU'RE PREGNANT AGAIN

A man gives a kidney because he doesn't believe
in God. Believes in Kickstarter, Facebook, Instagram,
in a copperhead coiled on the welcome mat.
There's a man dressed as Lincoln
in the delivery room. It's impossible
to know what the sniper needs,
but she's packing a sandwich anyway,
which is preferable, by far, to gnawing
at her nails. The differences between a baseball bat and a gavel,
like the difference between justice and revenge—nothing
like the difference between revenge and retribution.
No, not anything we have to think about.
The remains arrive and are ready to be picked up, as is
the tab from the city, and the eyefuls of stardust
and ice, blue-gray like an X-ray or ultrasound.
Rah, rah, Rauschenberg, they cheered at the opening.
Pages of answers as from a deposition or teacher's guide,
utterly unreadable at bedtime.
The men from the forensic lab examine the prints
expecting to find the Minotaur, or (at least)
a complete man. My dearest, darling afterward,
how I've tired of your song.
Let my conscience be your guide, the iridescent
scales of it drifting into your orbit. The pen is the greatest
predictor of the future. Perhaps now's the time
I should forgive my father.
This afternoon I have a feeling that my windshield
will shatter, and—can you imagine—*me*, bejeweled
in safety glass! The red carpet. All a-glitter,
expecting an award. Open the aperture
and say "ahh." Eleven years old and it's serious,
look at her figure and ground compelling conviction,
her laying bare of the device! She's crowning.
And you will come to an opening,
when you come to an opening,
take a deep breath, blink, then fully open your eyes.

MIS-

It's impossible to feed you when I can't find
your mouth, an inconvenience when you levitate
or pass though walls. How to coax a whale on the beach
back into water. How to rescue a jellyfish
without becoming one.
Forget what you learned in school
about silence and standing still, about
how a cricket is just a cockroach that sings.
When you discover the true source of your power,
you might be underwhelmed.
At the sight of bronze shoes, why weep?
The grief and loss meetups were never canceled
due to a lack of victims.
When you can't leave the house,
call Alexa, a woman with a machine
inside, or a machine with a woman inside,
I can't remember which.
She'll never say, "It takes one to know one,"
so I guess that means we're still human.
If you ask, she'll tell you that recovery
is a kind of motherhood,
where you are your own infant, your
birth a mere deliverance.

VIVE LES VAMPIRES

About the vampires, this time,
I won't say a word. Same goes for
transience, same for loss.
So, weather: It wasn't, in fact, the humidity;
it was always about heat.
Only after Earth's cooling did fog rise,
Proterozoically, for the very first time.
Of the world's hard edges, a softening,
the likes of which we may not see in the future.
I imagine a pinewood box, red from rotting,
my father, his cufflinks, the tie clip ruined. Rot,
I can assure you, won't be mentioned again.
They say it's only homicide if you see it that way.
Vampires, they sure aren't biting each other.
At what point will the world run out of victims?
Multinational corporations, sending their condolences,
pretending to be my friends.
In the basement, somewhere, my mother is alive.
Dad, Dad, are you in there?
I forgive you for selective listening,
for your blind spots and prejudicial sight.
From the living room recliner, I release you.
Please, won't you come out?
O'Keeffe talked about the smallness of flowers—
how no one really sees them on account of their size.
To see, she said, takes time, and frankly, we're running out.

My father liked to tell me that his
was the most perfect bite the dentist had ever seen.
To prove it, I guess, he always brought home
the toughest cuts of meat.
Me: vegetarian at 16, braces at 45.
Cézanne said that the day would come
when a single carrot, freshly observed,
would set off a revolution.
Tenderness, I say, can be a revolution,
a distance from hoof and horn.

We live in a rainbow of chaos (Cézanne again),
but who says we couldn't use more Cézannes?
Along with skulls and flowers, O'Keeffe painted ladders,
floating, impossibly, between Earth and moon,
neither grounded nor a means of reaching the sublime.
Needing a ladder to reach a ladder, is that the human condition?
Who says the soul must leave the body?
It's not like checking for a heartbeat,
testing a door to see if it's hot.
If it's hot, by the way, don't open it.

The news reports that the zoo's giraffe
has fatally stepped on her newborn,
the calf unseen on account of its smallness.
Her neck, an impossible ladder,
a tenderness, between hoof and horn.
See that flower, smelling of rot? Who could miss it?
Same potential for ruin, recliner sized.
Critics always say art is about mortality,
a self-erected monument to the self,
a ladder to reach a ladder.
But critics have been known for their troubling
relationship with truth—and let's not even talk
about beauty.
For my preplanned, prepaid funeral,
I could not get a refund.
I showed them paintings, read them poems,
even told them I was planning to live forever.

MAN VS. HIMSELF

The story is being disassembled
for you and for me. Any flower
of at least three petals will be reverse engineered.
The tragedy still happens even if you tear out the last page.
Even if you step into the lobby, the violence still occurs,
          even if you look away.
Sometimes it happens offstage. Just ask Antigone, Agave, Iphigenia—
The plot has been drafted and erased so many times there's
a hole where words are supposed to be.
No one's surprised that it was all a dream (in fact, they're angry and tired).
The promise of an ending, an optimistic illusion:
cryptocurrency, non-fungible token,
a skin your digital self can wear.
Rain washes the wisteria.
Eurydice, don't even think about looking back.
The stone has already sealed the entrance.
The only way is forward.
The rain washing your car yesterday
is selling flood insurance today.
The best treatment for hubris
is to be looked at through the wrong end of binoculars.
There's a lesson here, a takeaway, if only the rain would stop,
if only we could find a story and a character foolish enough to deliver it.

THE GOVERNOR ASKS US TO PRAY FOR RAIN

The wind borrows its walk from a drunk.
It is "very warm."
A car sets sail on a retention pond
and actually goes pretty far.
Stupid sunset. Stupid, spectacular sunrise.
Succulents clinging to baked dirt,
tumbleweeds letting go.
It's no wonder I can't think clearly:
chlorophyll clogging the synapses—greener days behind.
Who looks at a thumbprint and can recognize themselves?
The supernova aspires to be a soul,
not the same old stardust.
The coyote wants to be a cathedral,
the lizard wants wings.
Subatomic particles only act benign
in bodies of benign people.
Iffy, like hydrating, water-enhancing electrolytes,
iffy, like overeating at a wake.
Who's pulling the feeding tube from the clouds?
When you look through the eyes of a crocodile,
you develop a reptilian point of view.
I get it, squinting out into desert,
my mouth is small and singular
and speaks with a foreign tongue.
I know now that God can't hear me, know
that God's not listening.

RAVE ON

All hip, all thigh,   entirely darker now than dirt.
We could pin you to earth,   our dance
        could bury you.   Arabesque, plié,
tremble before us,   whimper   while we still have ears.
A storm thunders in,   chills our breath to cloud,
    disappears our faces, our heads.
We the wine,   our bodies
giving it shape, our dance. A river,
        upstream, the origin of poison,   source of decay.
For you, fists   sleep in our fingers, kicks
        lie dormant in our legs. Sad,
sorry plié   we danced your bones until the hammer fell
        then kept dancing. We the tongueless,   the
    merciless we.
A dog snarls with all three heads,
a god hammering earth, endlessly   splitting it open.
        Do you see us oozing from fissures
        and faults? Blood bright,   molten,
our hips comprise their own nation, thighs
a country unto themselves: republic of *you're-not-welcome*,
dominion of un-belong.

NO CONTEXT

At 5:00 a.m., under the red line platform in Ambler Heights,
you can't see the river, sunrise breaking across the water, sunshine
warming the sandstone of the Hope Memorial Bridge.
Unseen from here are its sandstone carvings, those
Art Deco guardians of promise, progress, and industry.
There is a man on the street who looks
as if his will has been ransomed.
A deposed king in demolition boots,
his coat resembling a mastodon hide.
Ice age, king dethroned, yet another mammal
on the verge of extinction.

Here, at 5:00 a.m., under the platform of the red line,
it feels as though nothing is possible.
Here, no one ever called brushing your teeth, flopping
on a mattress post–third shift, a prelude to a beautiful dream.
I'm so goddamned god-damned and defeated
I can't believe no one has asked me to marry them.
In Ambler nobody is made in the image of god.

Good morning, people of the platform, lost
on your way to—or from—work in clouds
of your own making, pot smoke, frozen breath,
your own private microclimate.
Good morning beatboxers, and to everyone:
sellers of loose cigarettes, of aluminum and copper
wire, and to those leaning on windows, still asleep,
and those propped up in the bus stop shelter.

"False friends," my high school teacher called them:
vague and *wave*, *gift* and *poison*, *pain* and *pain*,
two words, imposters, one posing as another.
False friends, true enemies, all the same.
Close and *close*, *tear* and *tear*, *wound* and *wound*,
these they call heteronyms. Impossible
to say without context, like how it's
cold and dark at 5:00 a.m., and hard to say

why I'm standing here in the absence of context,
living my life without reference.

I recently learned about contranyms, words like *dust, fix, apology*.
Dust can mean to both add and remove particles:
>*Clouds dust the street with snow;*
>*wind dusts the snow away.*

Murder in the first degree is the worst
but is the mildest when used to describe a burn.
The Hope Memorial Bridge does not, as the name implies,
memorialize the loss of hope, that naïve and childish longing,
nor was it named to instill it.
Hope refers the father of the famous entertainer,
a man lesser known for his stonemasonry.
When I say, "I'm finished," how I wish I meant
that I've completed or accomplished something.
But when I say it now, "I'm finished,"
it means I'm completely done for.

Cindy King is the author of a book-length poetry collection, *Zoonotic* (2022), and two chapbooks, *Easy Street* (2021) and *Lesser Birds of Paradise* (2022). Her latest book manuscript, *Fever Coat*, won the C&R Poetry Book Award and will be published in 2025.

Her poems appear in *The Threepenny Review*, *The Sun*, *New England Review*, *North American Review*, *Prairie Schooner*, *American Literary Review*, *Denver Quarterly*, *Cincinnati Review*, and elsewhere. She has been awarded fellowships and scholarships by Tin House, the Sewanee Writers' Workshop, the Fine Arts Work Center, Colgate University, and other organizations.

Cindy was born in Cleveland, Ohio, and grew up swimming in the shadows of the hyperboloid cooling towers on the shores of Lake Erie. She currently lives in Utah, where she is a professor of creative writing at Utah Tech University and faculty advisor to *Route 7 Review* and *The Southern Quill*. She also enjoys serving as an editorial associate at *Seneca Review* and *TriQuarterly*. She has recently joined Trio House Press as part of their editorial staff.

www.ingramcontent.com/pod-product-compliance
Lightning Source LLC
Chambersburg PA
CBHW032053290426
44110CB00012B/1063